ENGINEERING THE HUMAN BODY

# STEM CELLS

by Sue Bradford Edwards

T0014809

FOCUS
READERS

NAVIGATOR

# WWW.FOCUSREADERS.COM

Focus Readers is distributed by North Star Editions:
sales@northstareditions.com | 888-417-0195

Produced for Focus Readers by Red Line Editorial.

Content Consultant: In-Hyun Park, Associate Professor of Genetics, Yale University

Photographs ©: nobeastsofierce/Shutterstock Images, cover, 1; Gao bin/Imaginechina/AP Images, 4–5; Red Line Editorial, 7, 9; plenoy m/Shutterstock Images, 10–11; vetpathologist/Shutterstock Images, 13; Eugeneonline/iStockphoto, 15; James King-Holmes/Science Source, 17; Amélie Benoist/Science Source, 18–19; PavleMarjanovic/Shutterstock Images, 21; Paul Hakimata Photography/Shutterstock Images, 23; Corepics VOF/Shutterstock Images, 24–25; Ray Simons/Science Source, 26; Andy Crump/Science Source, 29

**Library of Congress Cataloging-in-Publication Data**
Names: Edwards, Sue Bradford, author.
Title: Stem cells / by Sue Bradford Edwards.
Description: Lake Elmo, MN : Focus Readers, [2020] | Series: Engineering the human body | Audience: Grades 4 to 6. | Includes bibliographical references and index.
Identifiers: LCCN 2018060037 (print) | LCCN 2019002592 (ebook) | ISBN 9781641859752 (PDF) | ISBN 9781641859066 (ebook) | ISBN 9781641857680 (hardcover) | ISBN 9781641858373 (pbk.)
Subjects: LCSH: Stem cells--Juvenile literature. | Embryonic stem cells--Juvenile literature. | Medical innovations--Juvenile literature. | Discoveries in science--Juvenile literature.
Classification: LCC QH588.S83 (ebook) | LCC QH588.S83 E388 2020 (print) | DDC 616.02/774--dc23
LC record available at https://lccn.loc.gov/2018060037

Printed in the United States of America
Mankato, MN
May, 2019

## ABOUT THE AUTHOR

Sue Bradford Edwards is a nonfiction author. She writes about many topics, including health, science, social studies, and history. Her books for young readers include *Meth, Steroids, The Zika Virus, Women in Science, The Dakota Access Pipeline, Evolution of Mammals,* and *Evolution of Reptiles.*

# TABLE OF CONTENTS

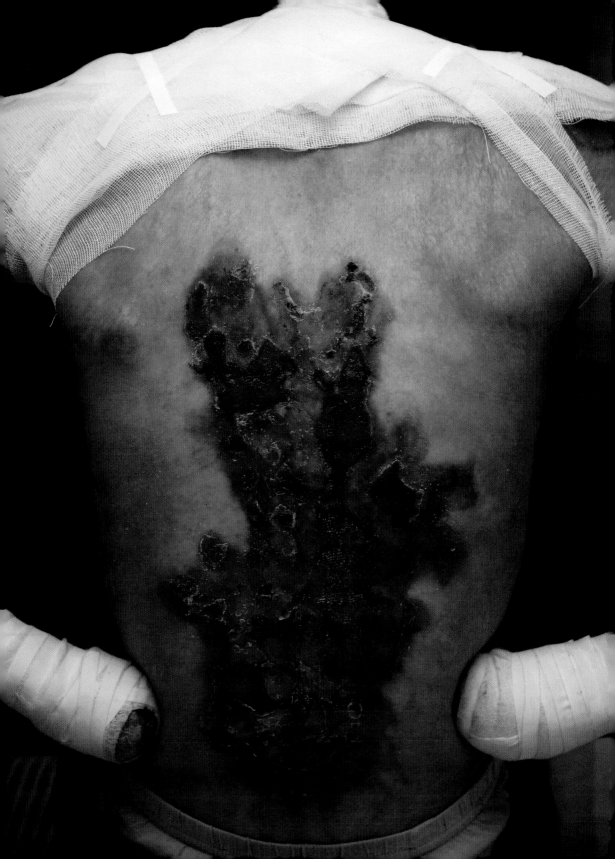

# CHAPTER 1

# NEW SKIN, NEW LIFE

**S**even-year-old Hassan had a deadly disease. It made his skin fall off. He blistered easily. By 2015, most of his skin was gone. He was in great pain. Doctors struggled to keep him alive. They decided to try an untested treatment. Usually treatments must go through strict testing. They must be proven to be safe.

Some skin diseases cause painful blisters and increase patients' chances of getting infections.

Only then can treatments be used on patients. But Hassan's treatment was allowed because he would die without it.

Doctors took cells from Hassan's remaining skin. They fixed the cells so the cells no longer had the disease. Then the doctors grew the cells into skin tissue. They did this using skin stem cells.

The body has many types of cells. They include muscle, bone, and blood cells. But stem cells are different. They are **unspecialized** cells. When a stem cell divides, the new cells can become stem cells. Or they can become other kinds of cells. This ability makes stem cells important. They can help the body heal.

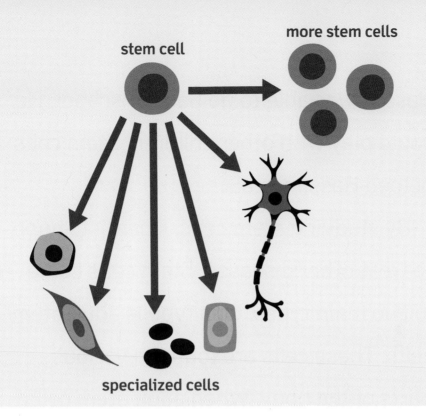

stem cell

more stem cells

specialized cells

Stem cells can divide and form more stem cells. They can also form specialized cells.

For example, Hassan's stem cells grew into healthy skin tissue. Doctors covered most of his body with the tissue. Over the next eight months, they watched his progress. The new skin attached to his body. It could heal from cuts and bruises.

Hassan was able to go back to school. He could play with other children. Stem cells helped Hassan heal.

By studying stem cells, scientists hope to treat other diseases. Stem cells come in two main types. One type is adult stem cells. These cells are found in various parts of the body. When adult stem cells divide, they can replace damaged cells. For example, adult stem cells in muscles can become new muscle cells.

The second type of stem cell is embryonic stem cells. An embryo is an organism at an early stage of growth. It contains stem cells that can become any other kind of cell. This flexibility makes embryonic stem cells valuable to scientists.

## STEM CELL DIFFERENCES

Embryonic stem cells can change into any other kind of cell. A whole human body forms from the stem cells of an embryo. Adult stem cells can only change into certain types of cells. For example, blood stem cells can only replace the types of cells found in the blood.

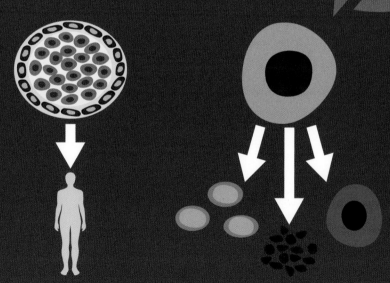

**EMBRYONIC STEM CELLS     ADULT BLOOD STEM CELL**

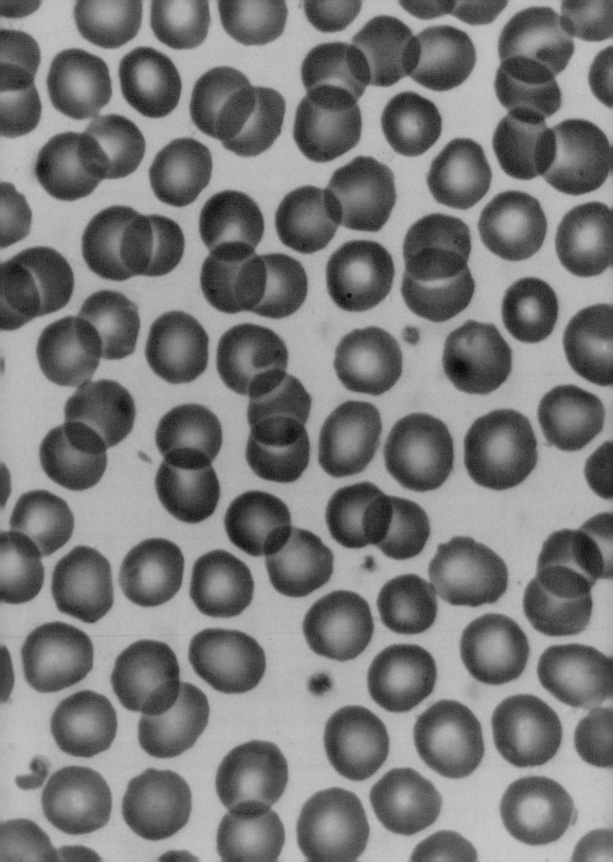

# CHAPTER 2

# STUDYING STEM CELLS

**A**lexander Maximow discovered stem cells in 1908. The Russian scientist was studying how blood cells divide. He saw that one type of cell could divide into red or white blood cells. He called this cell a stem cell.

Other scientists took stem cell research further. One was Dr. E. Donnall Thomas.

Scientists discovered stem cells during research into the division of blood cells.

This American scientist studied **bone marrow**. He wanted to cure leukemia. In this disease, bone marrow makes unhealthy blood cells. Thomas believed bone marrow **transplants** held the cure.

In 1956, Thomas had a patient with leukemia. The patient had an identical

## WHY STEM CELLS?

Ernst Haeckel was the first person to use the term *stem cell*. He was a German scientist born in the 1800s. He studied protozoa. They are single-celled organisms. Haeckel incorrectly believed that all life came, or stemmed, from protozoa. Because of this belief, he called them stem cells. In a 1909 report, Alexander Maximow used the same term. But he was describing blood stem cells.

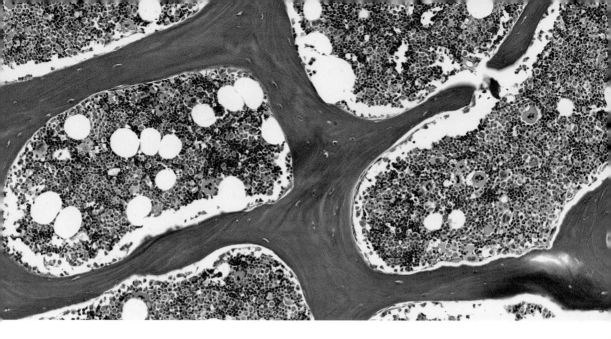

Stem cells in bone marrow can develop into the different types of blood cells.

twin. The twin donated bone marrow. Thomas transplanted it into his patient. The transplant was a success. The patient's body formed healthy blood cells.

Two Canadian scientists made the connection between bone marrow and stem cells. In 1960, they transplanted bone marrow cells into some lab mice.

Then they examined the mice. They found tiny bumps. There was one bump for each transplanted bone marrow cell.

The scientists studied each bump. They found early red and white blood cells. These cells would **mature** into red and white blood cells. The scientists realized they had found stem cells.

Stem cell research continued. In 2006, Japanese scientists were studying mouse skin cells. They inserted **genes** into each cell. The genes **reprogrammed** the cells. The cells didn't divide into more skin cells. They divided into embryonic stem cells. Scientists had turned specialized cells back into unspecialized stem cells.

Scientists are now able to make stem cells in a lab.

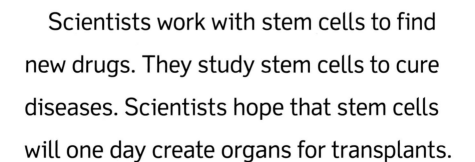

Scientists work with stem cells to find new drugs. They study stem cells to cure diseases. Scientists hope that stem cells will one day create organs for transplants.

# LAB-GROWN STEM CELLS

Scientists can now grow stem cells in labs. This process is called cell culture. Scientists grow cells in a plastic dish. They fill the dish with a nutrient-rich mixture. This mixture contains what the cells need to divide.

A good nutrient mixture is important. The wrong mixture will stop the stem cells from specializing. Specialized stem cells can help treat diseases. If bone marrow stem cells cannot specialize, they cannot produce blood cells. They cannot treat leukemia.

Scientists start by placing stem cells in the dish. Then the cells divide. New stem cells spread across the top of the mixture. A few embryonic stem cells can produce millions of new stem cells.

Scientists leave stem cells to grow until they are needed for experiments.

Lab-grown stem cells can be frozen. Then they can be shipped to other labs. Once thawed, they can grow new cells. Scientists use these cells in experiments.

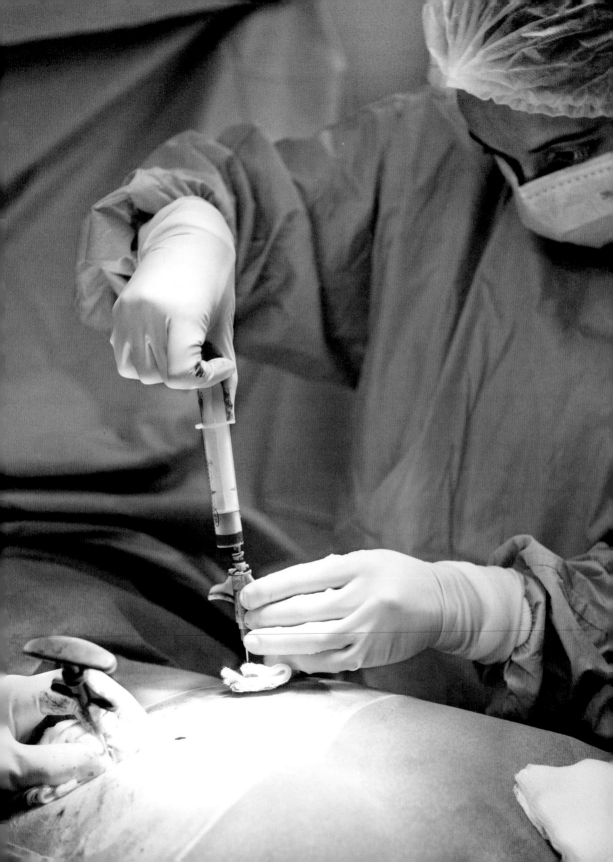

# CHAPTER 3

# USING STEM CELLS

Scientists use stem cells to treat many diseases. These treatments are collectively called stem cell therapy. The most common treatments are bone marrow transplants. These transplants treat leukemia. They can treat several other cancers, too. They also treat some blood diseases.

A doctor removes bone marrow for a transplant.

Cancer treatments can destroy bone marrow. After the treatments, the patient needs a bone marrow transplant. Bone marrow for transplants can come from two sources. It can come from a **donor**. It can also come from the patient.

In this second case, a doctor removes healthy bone marrow cells before the patient's cancer is treated. After the cancer treatments, the doctor returns the healthy cells to the patient through an IV tube. The healthy cells reach the bone marrow. There they make new blood cells.

Not all bone marrow transplants are successful. Sometimes transplanted cells attack healthy cells. The person's skin

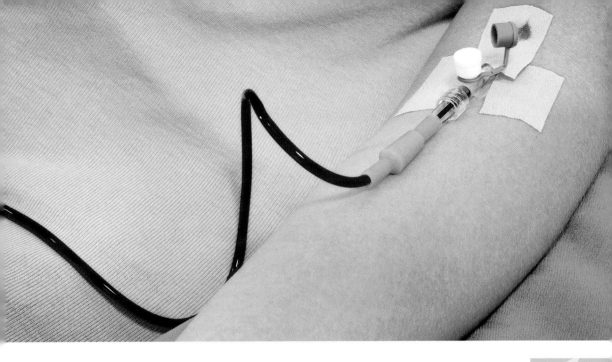

In a transplant, the bone marrow is injected directly into the patient's blood.

blisters. The patient bleeds internally. The patient can even die.

Mesenchymal stem cell therapy can help. The stem cells for this treatment come from bone marrow. The stem cells are frozen until needed. Once thawed, an IV carries the cells into the patient's blood. The stem cells improve healing.

They reduce swelling. They give the patient the chance to recover.

Other stem cells come from **umbilical cord** blood. After a baby is born, doctors can collect the blood from the cord. Scientists use the cells in research. The cells are like bone marrow stem cells.

## CONTROVERSY

Scientists often use embryonic stem cells in research. They **fertilize** human eggs in a lab. The cells divide. At the beginning of the third week, the cells are called an embryo. Removing the stem cells destroys the embryo. If an embryo continues to grow, it can become a baby. For this reason, some people are against this type of research.

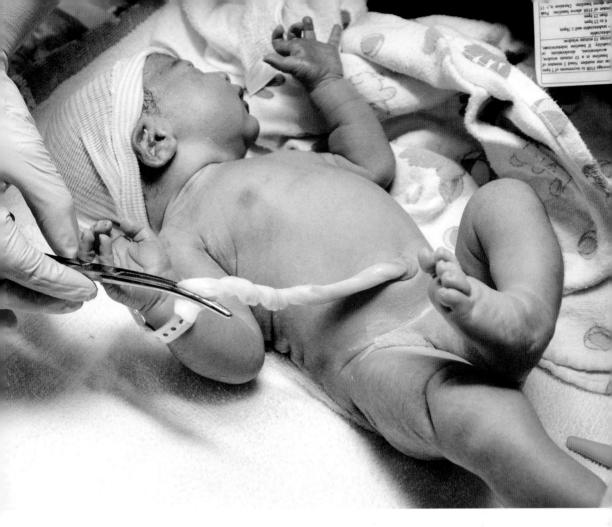

Scientists can harvest stem cells from the blood of umbilical cords.

They can be used to treat anyone. They can treat blood diseases. They can also help patients recover from cancer treatments.

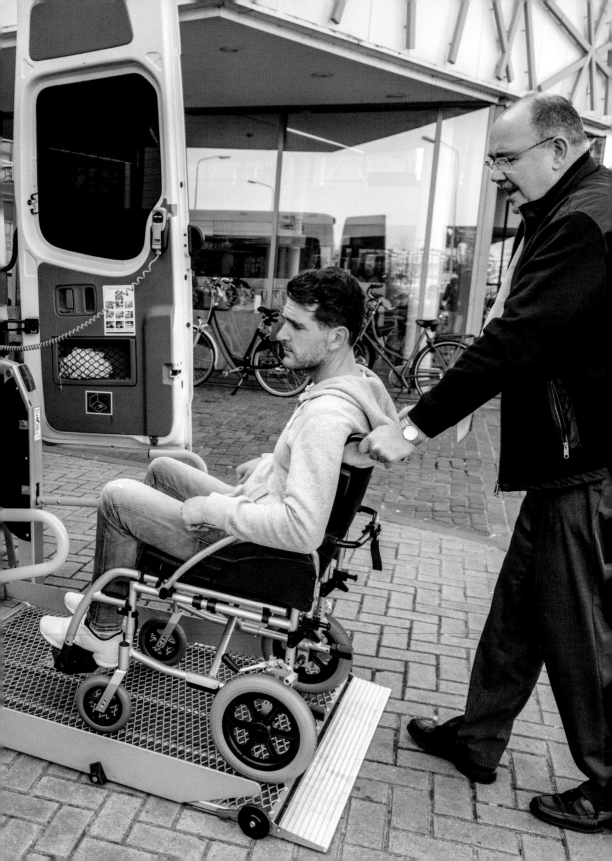

# CHAPTER 4

# FUTURE TREATMENTS

Scientists study stem cells to make new treatments. One goal is to mend the spinal cord. This bundle of nerves carries messages from the brain to the rest of the body. However, a back or neck injury can damage the spinal cord. This damage can cut off the flow of messages. It could leave the person unable to walk.

Spinal cord injury can result in loss of movement.

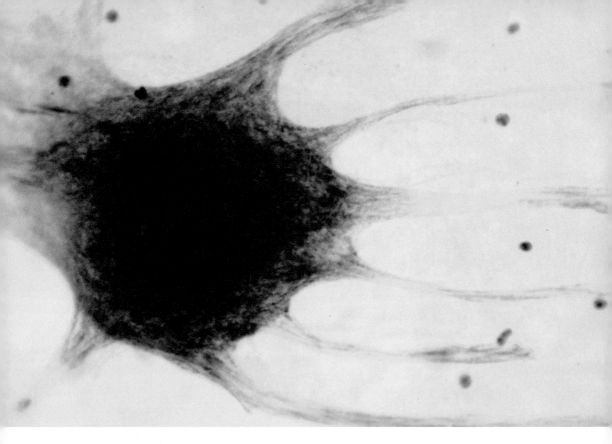

Nerve cells deliver messages between the brain and the rest of the body.

Scientists want to help people walk again. In experiments, scientists inject people with stem cells. They hope the stem cells will create new nerve cells. These cells could repair the spinal cord. Then the person would be able to walk.

Scientists also hope stem cells might someday cure type 1 diabetes. In this disease, patients' bodies do not make insulin. This chemical is needed to process sugar. Scientists have gotten stem cells to make insulin-producing cells in the lab.

## HEALED!

In June 2016, Jake Javier jumped into a swimming pool. He hit his head and was paralyzed. He couldn't move from the chest down. The next month, Jake took part in a stem cell trial. A doctor injected 10 million stem cells into his spinal cord. Jake can now use his arms and hands. Some of this progress could be natural healing. But Jake believes the stem cell therapy helped him heal.

However, more work is needed before people can be treated. One day, scientists will be ready to inject these cells into a human. The cells will make the insulin the person needs.

Scientists also want to grow whole new organs for transplant. But organs are complicated. They can't be grown in a dish. They need a frame.

In one experiment, scientists used hearts not suitable for transplant as frames. They removed parts of the cells of these hearts. They left cell walls and veins. These parts made frames. Scientists injected stem cells into the frames. After two weeks, heart cells had

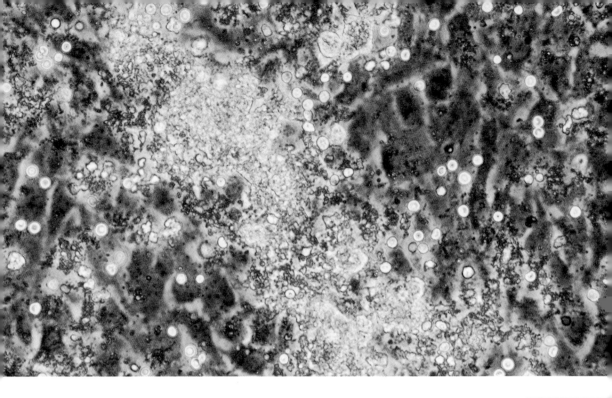

These heart muscle stem cells might one day be used to grow heart muscle for new organs.

grown from the stem cells. The resulting organs weren't complete hearts. But they could beat.

Scientists will continue studying stem cells. These unique cells may be the key to healing injuries. They may also help treat more diseases in the future.

# FOCUS ON
# STEM CELLS

*Write your answers on a separate piece of paper.*

1. Write a letter to a friend describing what you learned about stem cell therapy.

2. What do you think is the most important use for stem cells? Why?

3. What did Dr. E. Donnall Thomas do?

   **A.** He transplanted stem cells into mice.
   **B.** He used bone marrow to treat leukemia.
   **C.** He created embryonic stem cells.

4. What is one challenge for creating whole organs from stem cells?

   **A.** Lab-grown organs need frames.
   **B.** Stem cells do not divide easily.
   **C.** Lab-grown stem cells do not specialize.

*Answer key on page 32.*

# GLOSSARY

**bone marrow**
Soft, fatty material inside the bone where blood cells are created.

**donor**
A person who provides tissue or an organ for transplant.

**fertilize**
To cause an egg to begin developing into a new young animal or human.

**genes**
Tiny parts of cells that tell cells how to perform certain functions or that cause the body to develop certain traits.

**mature**
To become fully developed.

**reprogrammed**
Programmed again or differently.

**transplants**
Surgeries in which an organ or tissue sample is removed from one person and placed into another person's body.

**umbilical cord**
The flexible structure that connects a fetus to its mother.

**unspecialized**
Not used for a specific purpose.

# TO LEARN MORE

## BOOKS

Alkire, Jessie. *Medicine: From Hippocrates to Jonas Salk.* Minneapolis: Abdo Publishing, 2019.

Gibson, Karen Bush. *Cells: Experience Life at Its Tiniest.* White River Junction, VT: Nomad Press, 2017.

Marquardt, Meg. *Discover Cutting-Edge Medicine.* Minneapolis: Lerner Publications, 2017.

## NOTE TO EDUCATORS

Visit **www.focusreaders.com** to find lesson plans, activities, links, and other resources related to this title.

# INDEX

Answer Key: **1.** Answers will vary; **2.** Answers will vary; **3.** B; **4.** A